A daughter is
one of the most beautiful gifts
this world has to give.

Laurel Atherton

The "Language of" Series...

Thoughts to Share with a
WONDERFUL
DAUGHTER

A Blue Mountain Arts® Collection

Blue Mountain Press ™

SPS Studios, Inc., Boulder, Colorado

Library of Congress Catalog Card Number: 98-50181
ISBN: 0-88396-491-0

ACKNOWLEDGMENTS appear on page 48.

Certain trademarks are used under license.

Manufactured in Thailand
Fifth Printing: February 2001

 This book is printed on recycled paper.

Library of Congress Cataloging-in-Publication Data

Thoughts to share with a wonderful daughter : a Blue Mountain Arts collection.

    p. cm. -- ("Language of..." series)
  ISBN 0-88396-491-0 (alk. paper)
  1. Daughters--Literary collections. I. Series.
  PN6071.D3T49 1999
  808.81'93520441--dc21

                                98-50181
                                    CIP
                                    Rev.

SPS Studios, Inc.

P.O. Box 4549, Boulder, Colorado 80306

Contents

(Authors listed in order of first appearance)

To My Daughter,
I Love You

When you were born
I held you in my arms
and just kept smiling at you
You always smiled back
your big eyes wide open
full of love
You were such a
beautiful
good
sweet baby

Now
as I watch you grow up
and become your own person
I look at you
your laughter
your happiness
your simplicity
your beauty
And I know that you will
be able to enjoy a life
of sensitivity
goodness
accomplishment
and love
in a world that hopefully is at peace
I want to tell you that
I am so proud of you
and I dearly
love you

Susan Polis Schutz

If I Could, Daughter,
I'd Give You
All of Life's Best Gifts

If I could give you the best gifts of all, they would be the everlasting kind — like sunny thoughts to lift you high above your troubles and warm rays of love and friendship always in your heart. If I could shower you with happiness each hour, I would. If I could wrap you in protective ways, I would — making sure no problem ever touched your life or displaced your joy for living. If I could take your hand and lead you securely down life's path, safely shielding you from any harm, I would.

I'd do all this for you. If only the power were in my hands, I'd give you life's best gifts. But I hope you'll see that the very best gifts are truly yours already — beginning with your independent nature and the power to choose your own way to find happiness.

All the same, I'd like for you to know and remember this within your heart: I'm close by, caring for you greatly and wishing to protect you. My best gift to you, dear Daughter, will be as it has always been: my great love for you and my belief that you will choose your paths in life with honor and integrity, just as you always have.

Barbara J. Hall

If I hadn't had a child, I'd never have known that most elemental, direct, true relationship. I don't know if I'd fully understand the values of society that I prize. I would have missed some of the mystery of life and death. Not to know how a child grows, the wonder of a newborn's hand... I have been fortunate.

Dianne Feinstein

You are an exceptional person, and a *person* complete in your own right and must not seek reassurance of a kind which is not of your own fastidious standards.... It is a belief in your indomitable and singular talent which you must never compromise for others' approval, but follow your own star.

Kenneth Allsop
(Oct. 9, 1969 letter
to his daughter)

I Am Always Here for You, Daughter...

When you need someone
to talk to
I hope you will
talk to me
When you need someone
to laugh with
I hope you will
laugh with me
When you need someone
to advise you
I hope you will
turn to me
When you need someone
to help you
I hope you will
let me help you
I cherish and love
everything about you —
my beautiful daughter
And I will always support you
as a mother, as a person
and as a friend

Susan Polis Schutz

Of a Small Daughter
Walking Outdoors

Easy, wind!
Go softly here!
She is small
And very dear.

She is young
And cannot say
Words to chase
The wind away.

She is new
To walking, so
Wind, be kind
And gently blow

On her ruffled head,
On grass and clover.
Easy, wind...
She'll tumble over!

Frances M. Frost

A Flower Given
to My Daughter

Frail the white rose and frail are
Her hands that gave
Whose soul is sere and paler
Than time's wan wave.

Rosefrail and fair — yet frailest
A wonder wild
In gentle eyes thou veilest,
My blueveined child.

— James Joyce
from POMES PENYEACH
(Trièste, 1913)

You — the purest pleasure
of my life,
the split pit
that proves
the ripeness of the fruit,
the unbroken center
of my broken hopes —

O little one,
making you
has centered my lopsided life

so that if I know
a happiness
that reason never taught,
it is because of your small
unreasonably wrigglish
limbs.
Daughter, little bean,
sprout, sproutlet, smallest
girleen,
just saying your name
makes me grin.

I used to hate the word Mother,
found it obscene,
and now I love it
since that is me
to you.

Erica Jong

Children are the most wholesome part of the race, the sweetest, for they are freshest from the hand of God. Whimsical, ingenious, mischievous, they fill the world with joy and good humor. We adults live a life of apprehension as to what they will think of us; a life of defense against their terrifying energy; a life of hard work to live up to their great expectations. We put them to bed with a sense of relief — and greet them in the morning with delight and anticipation. We envy them the freshness of adventure and the discovery of life. In all these ways, children add to the wonder of being alive. In all these ways, they help to keep us young.

Herbert Hoover

My Favorite Woman

After we've spent the day together
we talk for hours on the phone
There is always more to say

She is the only person
I can comfortably shop with
and not feel impatient
when she tries on things forever
or worry that I'm taking too long
in deciding between two dresses

Only with her can I still giggle
mostly at the silliest things
I don't offer to shorten anyone else's hems
nor tidy up anyone else's kitchen
When she borrows something
I don't ask for it back

We exchange recipes
gossip about family members
and reminisce about the past

When she criticizes, it matters
Her compliments mean more
than those of friends

She is my favorite woman to be with
I am talking about my daughter.

Natasha Josefowitz

Mothers of daughters
are daughters of mothers
and have remained so, in
circles joined to circles,
since time began. They
are bound together by
a shared destiny.

Signe Hammer

Thou art thy mother's glass, and she in thee
Calls back the lovely April of her prime.

William Shakespeare

What the daughter does, the mother did.

Jewish Proverb

When the nurse brought my baby in, I looked into her face and saw myself — her eyes, her skin, her expressions, her spirit. She looked up at me and smiled her first hello. A broad and mischievous grin lit up her face, a sign that told me in no uncertain terms that this was a child to be reckoned with, a child who would be worthy of great things. From that moment on my heart was all hers. I was terrified, elated, proud, and complete... all at once.... On that day... we began our wonderful duet, a blend of heart, mind, and soul that continues to this day.

— Naomi Judd

Like one, like the other
Like daughter, like mother.

Anonymous

Fathers and Daughters...

Certain it is that there is no kind of affection so purely angelic as that of a father to a daughter. He beholds her both with and without regard to her sex. In love to our wives there is desire; to our sons there is ambition; but in that to our daughters there is something which there are no words to express.

Joseph Addison

When a father looks upon a daughter he bears the love that he bore her mother echoed down through the years.

Thomas Moore

Remember, dearest little daughter,
that you are your papa's only little girl
and that his first thought is always
and ought to be about you. I never go
to sleep without asking all good angels,
and especially one, to be near you.
You grow dearer and dearer to me the
farther I go away from you.

James Russell Lowell

The lucky man has a daughter as his first child.

Spanish Proverb

In the early morning
I shake my head
to clear away the static
of the dream
the way my daughter
shakes the radio she holds
against her ear
as if it were a shell.
On the table between us
the sun spreads
its slow stain;
fog lifts
from the coffee;
a heart drifts out of reach
on the surface
of the milk.
Now my daughter takes the day
into her hand
like fresh-baked bread —
she offers me a piece.

Linda Pastan

Don't Try to Grow Up
Too Fast

Youth is like a
fresh flower in May.
Age is like a rainbow
that follows the storms of life.
Each has its own beauty.

— David Polis

Many daughters have done well,
But you excel them all.

Proverbs 31:29 (NKJV)

What Is a Girl?

Little girls are the nicest things that happen to people. They are born with a little bit of angel-shine about them, and though it wears thin sometimes, there is always enough left to lasso your heart — even when they are sitting in the mud, or crying temperamental tears, or parading up the street in Mother's best clothes.

A little girl can be sweeter (and badder) oftener than anyone else in the world. She can jitter around, and stomp, and make funny noises that frazzle your nerves, yet just when you open your mouth, she stands there demure with that special look in her eyes. A girl is Innocence playing in the mud, Beauty standing on its head, and Motherhood dragging a doll by the foot.

Girls are available in five colors — black, white, red, yellow, or brown — yet Mother Nature always manages to select your favorite color when you place your order. They disprove the law of supply and demand — there are millions of little girls, but each is as precious as rubies.

God borrows from many creatures to make a little girl. He uses the song of a bird, the squeal of a pig, the stubbornness of a mule, the antics of a monkey, the spryness of a grasshopper, the curiosity of a cat, the speed of a gazelle, the slyness of a fox, the softness of a kitten, and to top it all off He adds the mysterious mind of a woman.

Who else can cause you more grief, joy, irritation, satisfaction, embarrassment, and genuine delight than this combination of Eve, Salome, and Florence Nightingale? She can muss up your home, your hair, and your dignity — spend your money, your time, and your patience — and just when your temper is ready to crack, her sunshine peeks through and you've lost again.

Yes, she is a nerve-racking nuisance, just a noisy bundle of mischief. But when your dreams tumble down and the world is a mess — when it seems you are pretty much of a fool after all — she can make you a king when she climbs on your knee and whispers, "I love you best of all!"

Alan Beck

A Daughter Is...

...a star glimmering in the sky
a wonder, a sweetness
a perception, a delight...
everything beautiful
A daughter is
love

— Susan Polis Schutz

...your greatest source of pride and
your greatest hope for the future...
The happiest moment of your life
was the day she was
introduced to the world.

— Bettie Meschler

...the companion, the friend, the confidant
of her mother... and the object of a
pleasure, something like the love between
angels, of her father.

— Sir Richard Steele

...a miracle that never
　　　ceases to be miraculous...
full of beauty
　　　and forever beautiful...
loving and caring
　　　and truly amazing.

— Deanna Beisser

...one of the most beautiful gifts
this world has to give.

— Laurel Atherton

...a bundle of firsts that excite and delight,
giggles that come from deep inside and are
　　　always contagious,
everything wonderful and precious,
and your love for her knows no bounds.

— Barbara Cage

...a wish come true.

— Kelly Lise

Advice to Daughter...

Do all the good you can,
By all the means you can,
In all the ways you can,
In all the places you can,
At all the times you can,
To all the people you can,
As long as ever you can.

John Wesley

Finish every day and be done with it. For manners and
for wise living it is a vice to remember. You have done what
you could; some blunders and absurdities no doubt crept in;
forget them as soon as you can. To-morrow is a new day;
you shall begin it well and serenely, and with too high a
spirit to be cumbered with your old nonsense. This day is
all that is good and fair. It is too dear, with its hopes and
invitations, to waste a moment on... yesterdays.

Ralph Waldo Emerson
(From a letter to his daughter)

Things to worry about:

    Worry about courage

    Worry about cleanliness

    Worry about efficiency

    Worry about horsemanship

    Worry about...

Things not to worry about:

    Don't worry about popular opinion

    Don't worry about dolls

    Don't worry about the past

    Don't worry about the future

    Don't worry about growing up

    Don't worry about anybody
      getting ahead of you

    Don't worry about triumph

    Don't worry about failure unless
      it comes through your own fault

    Don't worry about mosquitoes

    Don't worry about flies

    Don't worry about insects in general

    Don't worry about parents

    Don't worry about boys

    Don't worry about disappointments

    Don't worry about pleasures

    Don't worry about satisfactions

Things to think about:

    What am I really aiming at?

    How good am I really in
comparison to my contemporaries
in regard to:

    (a) Scholarship

    (b) Do I really understand about
people and am I able to get along
with them?

    (c) Am I trying to make my
body a useful instrument or am I
neglecting it?

— F. Scott Fitzgerald
(August 8, 1933 letter
to his daughter)

That I not be a restless ghost
Who haunts your footsteps as they pass
Beyond the point where you have left
Me standing in the newsprung grass,

You must be free to take a path
Whose end I feel no need to know,
No irking fever to be sure
You went where I would have you go....

So you can go without regret
Away from this familiar land,
Leaving your kiss upon my hair
And all the future in your hands.

Margaret Mead

The family is the one safe island
in an unknown sea.

Russian Proverb

Daughter...

Within you is an ideal,
a voice of youth,
and a promise of achievement
still to come.
Within your hands
are special gifts and talents.
Within your mind is the
source of your dreams.
Within you is the strength to carry
your dreams to completion.
Within your heart is the desire
to meet the world on your own terms,
and I never doubt that you will.
You are strong; you are wise;
you have a dream.
You have a spirit and confidence
I never knew;
you have faith.
You are your own person,
and you always will be.
Within you is something
so precious and rare.
Within you is the promise
of the future,
and I believe in you.

Jean Lamey

You have powers you never dreamed of.
You can do things you never thought you
could do. There are no limitations in what
you can do except the limitations in your
own mind as to what you cannot do.

Don't think you cannot.

Think you can.

— Darwin P. Kingsley

Never lose an opportunity of seeing anything that is beautiful.... Welcome [beauty] in every fair face, in every fair sky, in every flower, and thank God for it as a cup of blessing.

— Ralph Waldo Emerson

Do not follow where
the path may lead.
Go, instead, where there is no path
and leave a trail.

Anonymous

Outgrown

It is both sad and a relief to fold so carefully
her outgrown clothes and line up the little worn shoes
of childhood, so prudent, scuffed and particular.
It is both happy and horrible to send them galloping
back tappity-tap along the misty chill path into the past.

It is both a freedom and a prison, to be outgrown
by her as she towers over me as thin as a sequin
in her doc martens and her pretty skirt,
because just as I work out how to be a mother
she stops being a child.

Penelope Shuttle

Always Believe in Yourself, Daughter
...and Know That You Are Loved

Know yourself —
what you can do
and want to do in life
Set goals
and work hard to achieve them
Have fun every day in every way
Be creative —
it is an expression of your feelings
Be sensitive in viewing the world
Believe in the family
as a stable and rewarding way
of life
Believe in yourself
as you make choices
about your life
while following your dreams
Believe that you are
an important part of
everyone's life that you touch
Believe in love
as the most complete
and important emotion possible
and always know that
you are loved
and admired
by your family

Susan Polis Schutz

To My Daughter

Bright clasp of her whole hand around my finger,
My daughter, as we walk together now.
All my life I'll feel a ring invisibly
Circle this bone with shining: when she is grown
Far from today as her eyes are far already.

Stephen Spender

Home is the sacred refuge of our life.

John Dryden

A Little Light

In that dark, lonesome place
between a dream dreamed
and a dream realized,

I have left a little light for you
so you will know that someone cares
and believes in your dream.

Just where it becomes the most dark
and difficult to find your way,
there is the light I left for you.

It will light your way through the doubt,
the confusion, and the fears.

It will stay with you all the way
to the realization of your dream.

And when your dream has come true,
please go back to that darkest place
where you have been,
and set the little light there
to give heart to the next trembling soul
that braves the path to its dreams.

Mikki Brain

Daughter, my memories of you
    always take me back through the years...
memories of an infant
    so sweet and small and trusting,
memories of a toddler
    giggling with the joy of childhood,
memories of a young girl smiling
    and playing with her friends,
memories of your teen years
    full of change and doubt and growth.

My memories of you
mark your journey from a baby to a girl
and, magically, to a beautiful young lady.
I cannot believe that the time
    has passed so quickly...

Though miles and schedules keep us apart,
our bond exceeds distance and time.
Life is a blessing with you by my side,
    with you always in my heart.

Darlene Helms Griffin

How lonely the house seems — I never knew before how well you helped to fill it…. Ever since you went away, I have been wondering if it was as hard for you to go out into the world as it was for me to have you go.

Don't write short, hurried letters, simply stating facts in their tersest form, but tell me all your thoughts and dreams and plans, your worries and trials, and we will talk them over as two comrades…. If there is anything in my life that can be of value to you, I want you to have it; if I can save you a stumble or a single false step, I want to do it, but the only way I can do it is to know your heart.

Florence Wenderoth Saunders

I think of you a great deal. I bring home a great many beautiful flowers, — roses and poppies and lilies and bluebells and pinks and many more besides, — but it makes me feel sad to think that my little (daughter) cannot see them.

Nathaniel Hawthorne

Daughter

Ever so gently
   I hold you in my hands
   beautiful butterfly.

Diaphanous wings
   gently test the breeze
   promise predestined flight.

A fragment of time passes
   such a short time it seems
   to the hands that hold you close.

Gossamer wings
   grow strong
   and restless.

The morning comes when you leave my hands
   and flutter triumphantly around me
   though remaining quite near
   a mere breath away.

Each new day you venture further
    perfect, powerful wings
    carry you away from my protective hands
    as you seek the wind
    yet return at the coming of night.

This day, though, my proud heart rejoices
    this day my bursting heart
        silently weeps.

    This splendid butterfly soars aloft
    to touch cerulean skies
    to discover her own laughter and joy,
    triumph and pain,
    free, unfettered, unique.

    No longer in need
        of these hands that have held you,
    but forever cradled
        in my heart.

Elizabeth Hall

For My Grown-Up Daughter

It seems like yesterday
I tucked you in at night,
whispering a prayer of thanks
for another day of
having you in my life.

Not so long ago,
we were putting your baby teeth
out for the tooth fairy,
and reading storybooks
until you fell asleep in my arms.
It felt as though
you grew overnight
into a beautiful young lady.

Today, Daughter,
I see you reaching out to people,
showing that one person
can make a difference in this world.
And what a difference you've made!
I know my life could never have been so
full and complete without you being
such an important part of it.
I've watched the difference you've made
in the lives of others as well.
You have a very special gift
that inspires people to be
the best they can be.
I'm so proud of all that you do,
and I hope you'll never forget that
I love you with all my heart!

Carol Was

To Daughters...

I want my daughters to be beautiful, accomplished, and good; to be admired, loved, and respected, to have a happy youth, to be well and wisely married, and to lead useful, pleasant lives.

— Louisa May Alcott

I long to put the experience of fifty years at once into your young lives, to give you at once the key of that treasure chamber every gem of which has cost me tears and struggles and prayers, but you must work for these inward treasures yourselves.

— Harriet Beecher Stowe,
writing to her twin daughters

Happiness cannot come from without.
It must come from within. It is not what we
see and touch or that which others do for
us which makes us happy; it is that which
we think and feel and do, first for the other
fellow and then for ourselves.

— Helen Keller

Daughter, You Are
in My Heart Forever

The first time I held you in my arms
and you wrapped your tiny hand
around my index finger, I felt my heart
swell with immeasurable joy and pride.
I knew that my life had been touched in
a miraculous way that would transform
every dimension of it forever.

From the moment you were born,
you became the focal point of my
existence. Your smile was the sunshine
in my heart. Your happiness was the
only treasure I sought.

And so began the great paradox of
parenthood. For when your tiny hand
touched mine, I knew that I had been
chosen to nurture you, love you, and
then give you the strength to let go.

Letting go is not easy. But I look at you now — a beautiful young woman, strong in your convictions and determined to face life on your own terms — and I still feel my heart swell with pride and joy.

My dreams for your life might not always be the same ones you seek. But one thing remains the same: your happiness will always be my greatest treasure. I know now that the true miracle of that first touch lies in one simple truth: even though your hand may slip away from mine, we will hold each other in our hearts forever.

Nancy Gilliam

In your happiest and most exciting moments, my heart will celebrate and smile beside you.

In your lowest lows, my love will be there to keep you warm, to give you strength, and to remind you that your sunshine is sure to come again.

In your moments of accomplishment, I will be filled so full of pride that I may have a hard time keeping the feeling inside of me.

In your moments of disappointment, I will be a shoulder to cry on, and a hand to hold, and a love that will gently enfold you until everything's okay.

In your gray days, I will help you search, one by one, for the colors of the rainbow.

In your bright and shining hours, I will be smiling, too, right along beside you.

In your life, I wish I could give you a very special gift. It would be this:

When you look in the mirror in the days ahead, may you smile a hundred times more than frowning at what you see.

Smile because you know that a loving, capable, sensible, strong, precious person is reflected there.

And when you look at me, may you remember how very much I love you... and how much I'll always care.

 Laurel Atherton

To My Beautiful Daughter,
I Love You

You are a shining
example of what a
daughter can be —
loving and compassionate
beautiful and good
honest and principled
determined and independent
sensitive and intelligent
You are a shining
example of what every
parent wishes their
daughter were
and I am so very
proud of
you

— Susan Polis Schutz

ACKNOWLEDGMENTS

We gratefully acknowledge the permission granted by the following authors, publishers, and authors' representatives to reprint poems or excerpts from their publications.

Dianne Feinstein for "If I hadn't had a child..." from STARRING MOTHERS by Jill Barber. Copyright © 1987 by Dianne Feinstein. All rights reserved. Reprinted by permission.

Viking Penguin, a division of Penguin Putnam, Inc., and the Estate of James Joyce for "A Flower Given to My Daughter" from JAMES JOYCE: POEMS AND SHORTER WRITINGS, Faber & Faber, London 1991. Copyright © 1918 by B. W. Huebsch, Inc., copyright © 1927, 1936 by James Joyce, copyright © 1946 by Nora Joyce, copyright © the Estate of James Joyce. All rights reserved. Reprinted by permission.

The Peters Fraser & Dunlop Group, Ltd. For "You are an exceptional person..." by Kenneth Allsop from LETTERS TO HIS DAUGHTER edited by Amanda Allsop. Copyright © 1974 by the Estate of Kenneth Allsop. Compilation and introduction Copyright © 1974 by Amanda Allsop. All rights reserved. Reprinted by permission of the Peters Fraser & Dunlop Group on behalf of the Estate of Kenneth Allsop.

Erica Jong for "You — the purest pleasure..." from ORDINARY MIRACLES by Erica Jong. Copyright © 1983 by Erica Jong. All rights reserved. Reprinted by permission.

Natasha Josefowitz for "My Favorite Woman." Copyright © 1986 by Natasha Josefowitz. All rights reserved. Reprinted by permission.

Villard Books, a division of Random House, Inc., for "When the nurse..." from LOVE CAN BUILD A BRIDGE by Naomi Judd. Copyright © 1993 by Naomi Judd. All rights reserved. Reprinted by permission.

Linda Pastan for "In the early morning...." Copyright © 1980 by Linda Pastan. All rights reserved. Reprinted by permission.

Scribner, a division of Simon & Schuster, Inc., and Harold Ober Associates, Inc. for "Things to worry about..." from F. SCOTT FITZGERALD: A LIFE IN LETTERS edited by Matthew J. Bruccoli. Copyright © 1994 by the Trustees under Agreement dated July 3, 1975, created by Frances Scott Fitzgerald Smith. All rights reserved. Reprinted by permission.

William Morrow & Co., Inc. for "That I not be a restless ghost..." from BLACKBERRY WINTER by Margaret Mead. Copyright © 1972 by Margaret Mead. All rights reserved. Reprinted by permission.

Random House, Inc. and Faber & Faber for "To My Daughter" from SELECTED POEMS by Stephen Spender. Copyright © 1955 by Stephen Spender. All rights reserved. Reprinted by permission.

Mikki Brain for "A Little Light." Copyright © 1999 by Mikki Brain. All rights reserved. Reprinted by permission.

Elizabeth Hall for "Daughter." Copyright © 1999 by Elizabeth Hall. All rights reserved. Reprinted by permission.

David Higham Associates for "Outgrown" from BUILDING A CITY FOR JAMIE by Penelope Shuttle, published by Oxford University Press. Copyright © 1996 by Penelope Shuttle. All rights reserved. Reprinted by permission.

A careful effort has been made to trace the ownership of poems and excerpts used in this anthology in order to obtain permission to reprint copyrighted materials and give proper credit to the copyright owners. If any error or omission has occurred, it is completely inadvertent, and we would like to make corrections in future editions provided that written notification is made to the publisher:

SPS STUDIOS, INC., P.O. Box 4549, Boulder, Colorado 80306.